JAMAICA BAY   VULNERABILITY FACTORS

JAMAICA BAY VULNERABILITY FACTORS

STRUCTURES OF COASTAL RESILIENCE
Jamaica Bay Team
Spitzer School of Architecture
The City College of New York

Catherine Seavitt Nordenson, editor
Associate Professor of Landscape Architecture

Kjirsten Alexander
Research Associate

Danae Alessi
Research Associate

Eli Sands
Research Assistant

JAMAICA BAY PAMPHLET LIBRARY
06 Jamaica Bay Vulnerability Factors

ISBN 978-1-942900-06-1

COPYRIGHT

CONTACT

Catherine Seavitt Nordenson
cseavittnordenson@ccny.cuny.edu
www.structuresofcoastalresilience.org

SCR Jamaica Bay Team
The City College of New York
Spitzer School of Architecture
Program in Landscape Architecture, Room 2M24A
141 Convent Avenue New York, New York 10031

COVER

Population Density and Race.
data source: US Census

supported by

   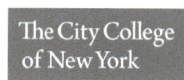

VULNERABILITY AT JAMAICA BAY

The US Army Corps of Engineers defines vulnerability as a function of the hazard to which a system is exposed, the sensitivity of the system to the hazard, and the system's adaptive capacity.* This project seeks to provide a fine-grained study of vulnerability at Jamaica Bay, closely examining USACE's Composite Risk Index by delaminating and geospatially mapping the layered indices of social, environmental, and infrastructural risk. Risk is defined by USACE as the potential for the realization of unwanted, adverse consequences. Climate change and sea level rise affects each of these categories, through possible loss of life and property from flooding, loss of valuable wetland ecologies, and loss of critical infrastructures such as transportation, power, and communication. The Jamaica Bay vulnerability maps provide a focused lens for assessing at-risk communities and ecologies.

*Ty Wamsley, Chief of the US Army Corps of Engineers' Flood and Storm Protection Division, Coastal and Hydraulics Laboratory, Engineer Research and Development Center. Vulnerability Metrics, September 25, 2013.

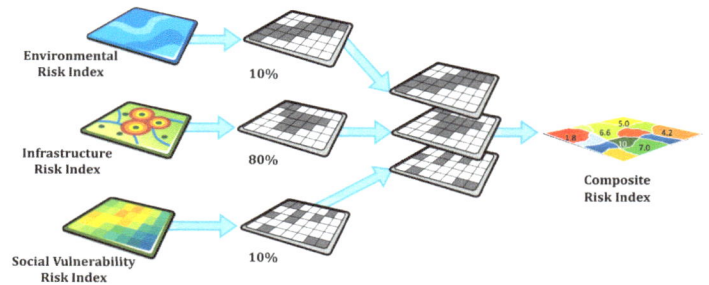

source: US Army Corps of Engineers process and percentiles for creating a Composite Risk Index, 2013

Rituals at North Channel Beach parking lot, looking north. c. 1998
photo: Don Riepe

SOCIAL VULNERABILITY AT JAMAICA BAY

Social vulnerability at Jamaica Bay is mapped through the use of 2010 US Census block and tract demographic data. Historic census tract data from the past four decades reveals how rapidly these demographics shift in New York City, and of course the demographics in the Jamaica Bay region will continue to change in the future. A dot-density method is used to create population and race maps which represent only people; no geographic features are used. This allows the demographic data to be viewed spatially to identify dense "hot spots" of vulnerability indices such as poverty and age. The dot-density mapping method often reveals unexpected patters of risk and vulnerability, and enables a prioritized assessment of local protective strategies for the most vulnerable populations.

DEMOGRAPHICS
1 DOT = 20 PEOPLE
● WHITE
● BLACK
● ASIAN
● HISPANIC
● OTHER

SOCIAL VULNERABILITY POPULATION AND RACE

data source: US Census

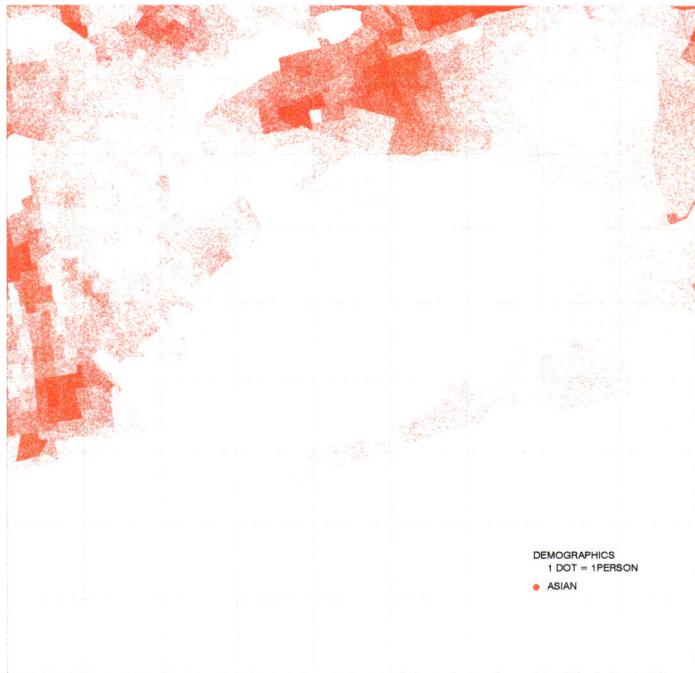

DEMOGRAPHICS
1 DOT = 1PERSON
● ASIAN

DEMOGRAPHICS
1 DOT = 1PERSON
● BLACK

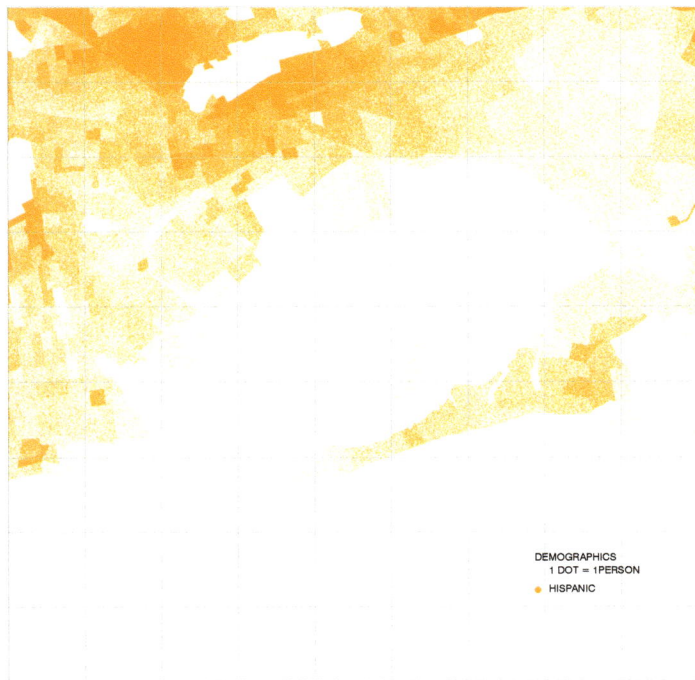

DEMOGRAPHICS
1 DOT = 1PERSON
● HISPANIC

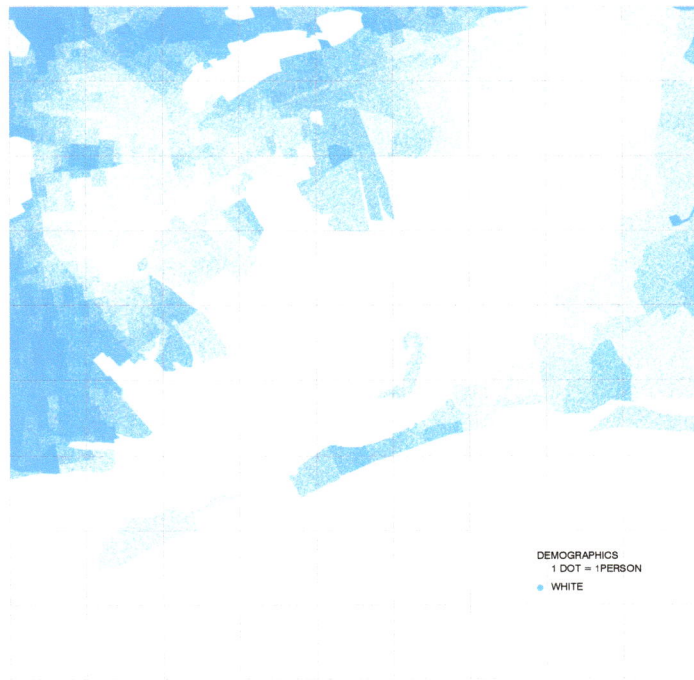

DEMOGRAPHICS
1 DOT = 1PERSON
● WHITE

DEMOGRAPHICS
  1 DOT = 5 PEOPLE
● FEMALE HEAD OF HOUSEHOLD WITH CHILDREN
● FEMALE 65+ AND ALONE
● MALE 65+ AND ALONE
● CHILDREN UNDER 5
● TOTAL POPULATION BELOW 125% OF POVERTY LINE
● DIFFICULTY SPEAKING ENGLISH

SOCIAL VULNERABILITY POPULATION AND RISK FACTORS

data source: US Census

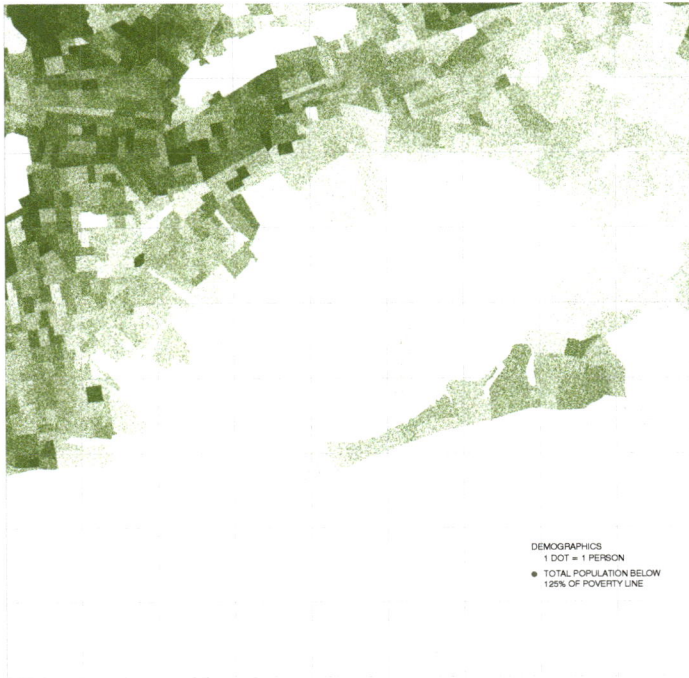

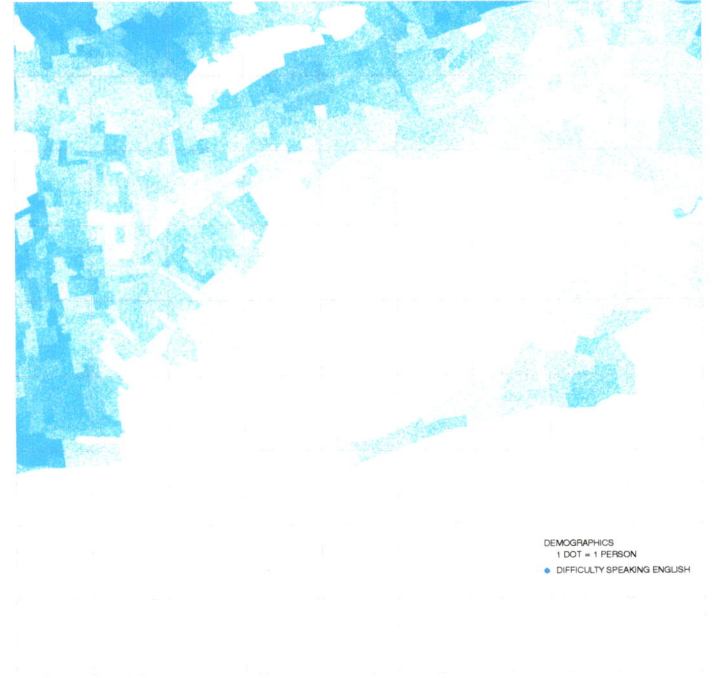

HURRICANE SANDY HINDCAST 2012

data source: Federal Emergency Management Administration

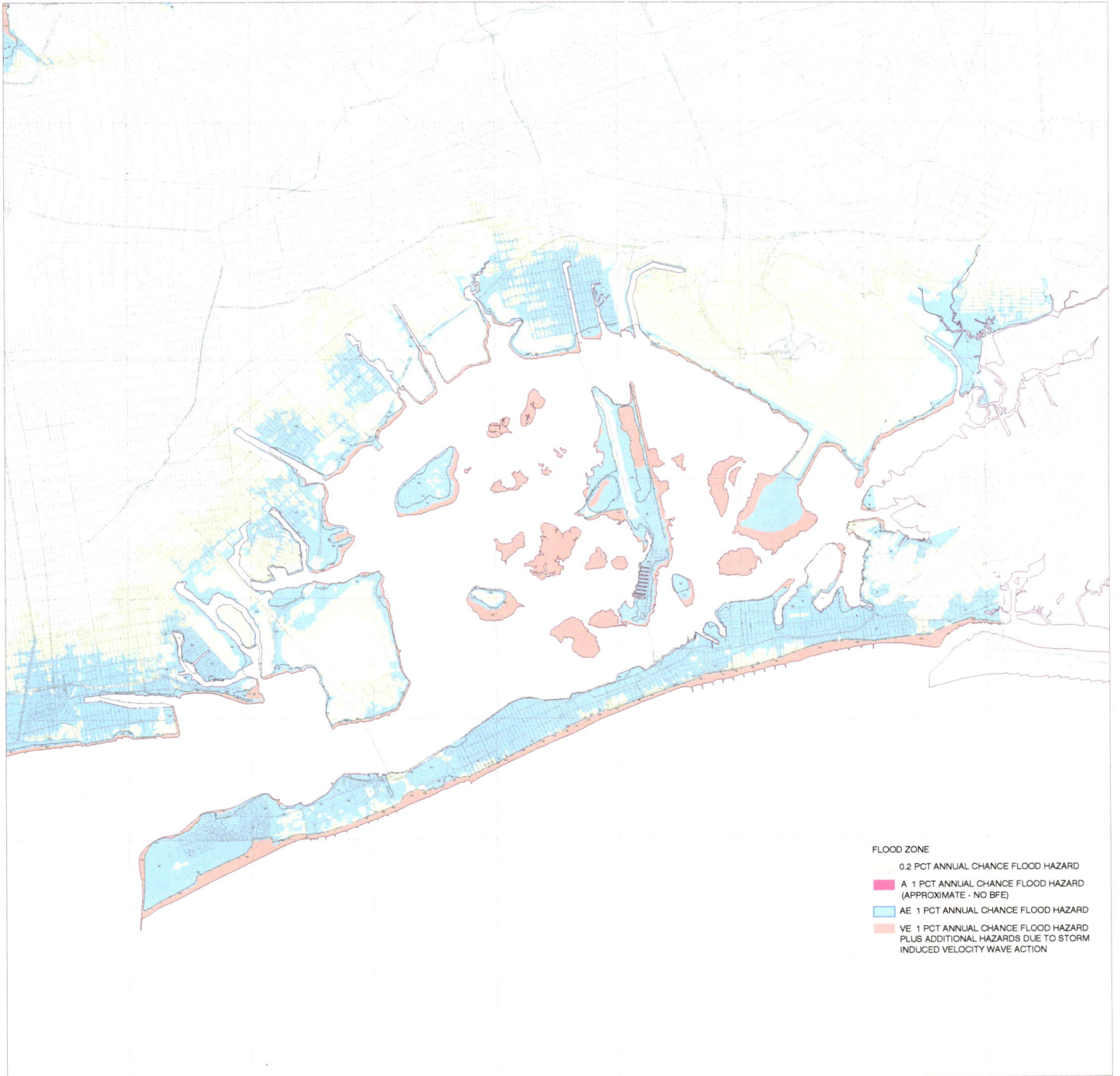

FLOOD ZONE

0.2 PCT ANNUAL CHANCE FLOOD HAZARD

A   1 PCT ANNUAL CHANCE FLOOD HAZARD
(APPROXIMATE - NO BFE)

AE 1 PCT ANNUAL CHANCE FLOOD HAZARD

VE 1 PCT ANNUAL CHANCE FLOOD HAZARD
PLUS ADDITIONAL HAZARDS DUE TO STORM
INDUCED VELOCITY WAVE ACTION

FEMA PRELIMINARY DIGITAL FLOOD INSURANCE RATE MAP DECEMBER 2013

data source: Federal Emergency Management Administration

ENVIRONMENTAL VULNERABILITY AT JAMAICA BAY

Salt marsh loss at Jamaica Bay is a paradigmatic example of environmental vulnerability, particularly given future sea level rise. A resilient marsh ecosystem provides coastal storm risk management services to adjacent communities through wind fetch reduction and wave attenuation. Addressing poor water quality and sediment starvation is necessary for the sustained performance of any environmental improvements at Jamaica Bay, but particularly for the future success (and indeed, the continued existence) of the salt marsh islands. The project also geospatially maps rare and sensitive ecosystems at Jamaica Bay by using NOAA's Environmental Sensitivity Index for at-risk shorelines. Vulnerable large tract ecosystems are located using the EPA's EnviroAtlas Macroform Rarity Index toolbox. Threatened and endangered plant and animal species are also identified and mapped.

Oystercatchers on Rockaway Beach
photo: Don Riepe

Collapse at marsh edge, Jamaica Bay Wildlife Refuge
photo: Don Riepe

LARGE TRACT ECOSYSTEMS

▨ APPALACHIAN HEMLOCK-HARDWOOD FOREST
▨ ATLANTIC COASTAL PLAIN NORTHERN MARITIME FOREST
▨ GULF AND ATLANTIC COASTAL PLAIN TIDAL MARSH SYSTEMS
▨ NORTHERN ATLANTIC COASTAL PLAIN DUNE AND SWALE

ENVIRONMENTAL VULNERABILITY ECOSYSTEMS

data source: US Environmental Protection Agency

Appalachian Hemlock-Hardwood Forest
photo: Don Riepe

Atlantic Coastal Plain Northern Maritime Forest
photo: Don Riepe

Gulf and Atlantic Coastal Plain Tidal Marsh System
photo: Don Riepe

Northern Atlantic Coastal Plain Dune and Swale
photo: Darae Alessi

SENSITIVE SHORELINE TYPE

FINE TO MEDIUM GRAINED SAND BEACHES

EXPOSED TIDAL FLATS

SALT & BRACKISH WATER MARSHES

ENVIRONMENTAL VULNERABILITY SHORELINES

data source: National Oceanic and Atmospheric Administration

Salt and Brackish Water Marshes
photo: Don Riepe

Salt and Brackish Water Marshes
photo: Don Riepe

Exposed Tidal Flats
photo: Don Riepe

Fine to Medium Grained Sand Beaches
photo: Don Riepe

Least tern
Common tern

Common tern
Least tern

Common tern

Common tern

Common tern

Least tern

Common tern
Least tern

Common tern

Common tern
Least tern

Common tern

Common tern

Seabeach amaranth

Piping plover

Black skimmer
Seabeach amaranth
Common tern

Piping plover
Piping plover

Piping plover
Piping plover
Least tern

Piping plover
Least tern

Peregrine falcon

Common loon

Least tern Common tern

Piping plover

Common tern
Least tern Roseate tern
Black skimmer

Piping plover

NOAA ENVIRONMENTAL SENSITIVITY INDEX MAP

THREATENED / ENDANGERED SPECIES

THREATENED PLANT

Present in Atlantic Ocean in NY
State Waters

Present in Jamaica Bay

Black rail

Fin whale

Leatherback sea turtle

Humpback whale

Loggerhead sea turtle

Leatherback sea turtle

Present in marshes in Jamaica Bay

Loggerhead sea turtle

Black rail

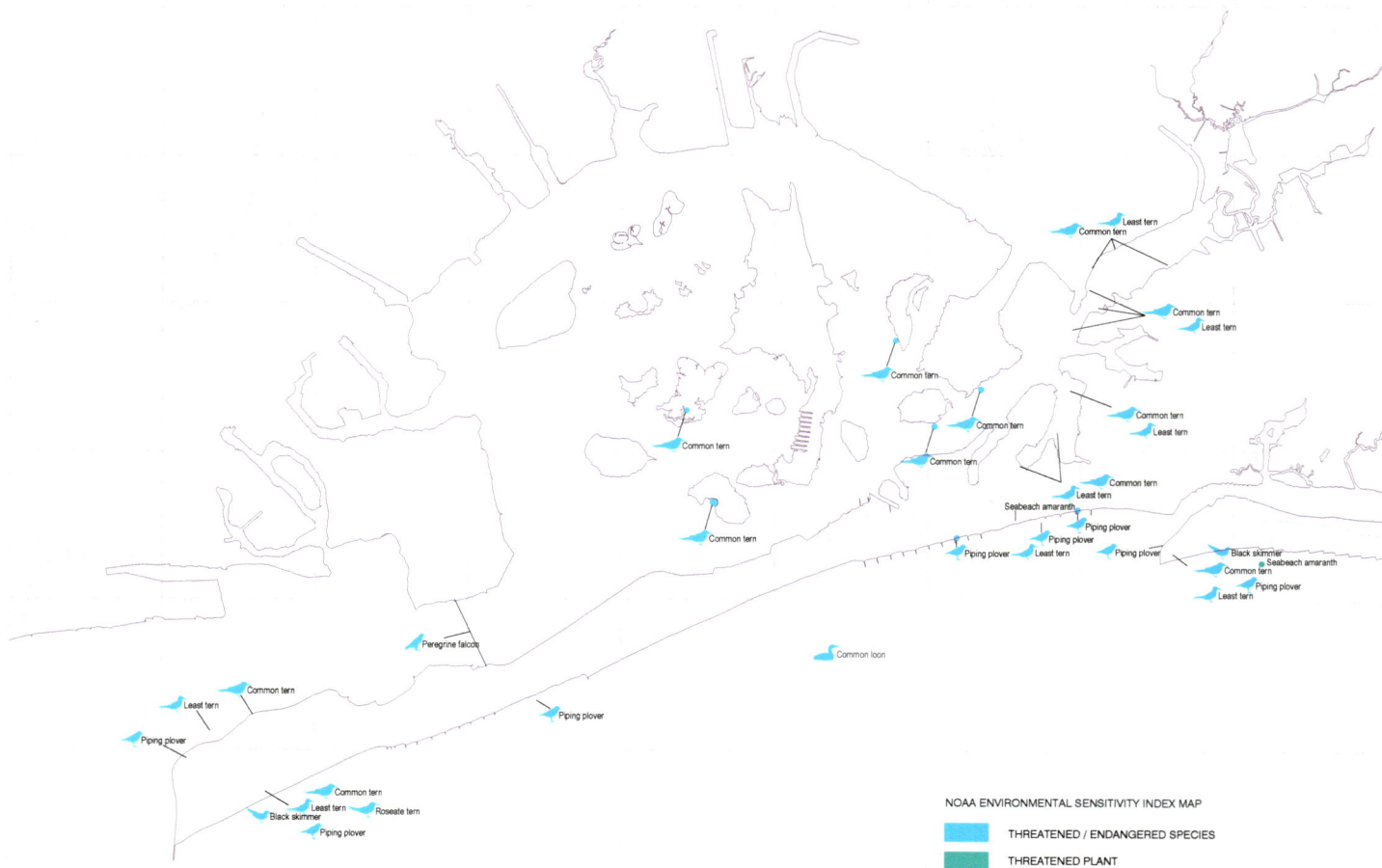

ENVIRONMENTAL VULNERABILITY THREATENED AND ENDANGERED SPECIES

data source: National Oceanic and Atmospheric Administration

Species	State /Federal	Threatened/ Endangered	Jan	Feb	Mar	Apr	May	Jun	Jul	Aug	Sep	Oct	Nov	Dec	Notes
Black rail	S	E					▬	▬	▬	▬	▬	▬			Present in Jamaica bay and marshes
Black skimmer	S	S					▬	▬	▬	▬	▬	▬			Nesting: May-Sept; present near Breezy Point ocean front and Atlantic Beach near western tip
Common loon	S	S	▬	▬	▬	▬	▬				▬	▬	▬	▬	Present in Atlantic Ocean
Common tern	S	T					▬	▬	▬	▬	▬	▬			Nesting: May-Sept; present near Breezy Point ocean front and NW near Rockaway Inlet, Little Egg, Yellow Bar, JoCo marsh, SE portion of Rockaway Community Park, JFK (SE), Inwood (NW), and Atlantic Beach near western tip
Least tern	S	T					▬	▬	▬	▬	▬				Present near Breezy Point ocean front (nesting May-Sept) and NW near Rockaway Inlet, SE portion of Rockaway Community Park, JKF (SE), Averne, Inwood (NW) and Atlantic Beach near western tip
Peregrine falcon	S	E	▬	▬	▬	▬	▬	▬	▬	▬	▬	▬	▬	▬	Nesting: May-Sept; present at Marine Parkway Gil Hodges Memorial Bridge
Piping plover	S/F	E/T				▬	▬	▬	▬	▬	▬	▬			Nesting: April-Aug; present near Breezy Point ocean front and NW tip near Rockaway Inlet, Jacob Riis ocean front, Arverne ocean front, Edgemere ocean front and Atlantic Beach near western tip
Roseate tern	S/F	E/E					▬	▬	▬	▬					Nesting: May-Aug; present near Breezy Point ocean front
Shortnose Sturgeon	S/F	E/E	▬	▬	▬	▬	▬	▬	▬	▬	▬	▬	▬	▬	Juveniles/Adults: Jan-Dec; present in Raritan Bay
Fin whale	S/F	E/E	▬	▬	▬	▬	▬	▬	▬	▬	▬	▬	▬	▬	Present in Atlantic Ocean in NY State waters, East River and Atlantic Ocean NJ State waters (April, Sept-Nov)
Humpback whale	S/F	E/E					▬	▬	▬	▬	▬	▬	▬		Present in Atlantic Ocean in NY State waters, East River and Atlantic Ocean NJ State waters (April, Sept-Nov)
Northern right whale	S/F	E/E					▬	▬				▬			Present in Atlantic Ocean in NJ State waters
Leatherback sea turtle	S/F	E/E							▬	▬	▬	▬			Present in Jamaica Bay, Atlantic Ocean (including NY/NJ State waters), Raritan Bay and East River (July-Sept)
Loggerhead sea turtle	S/F	T/T							▬	▬	▬	▬			Present in Jamaica Bay, Atlantic Ocean (including NY/NJ State waters), Raritan Bay and East River (July-Sept)

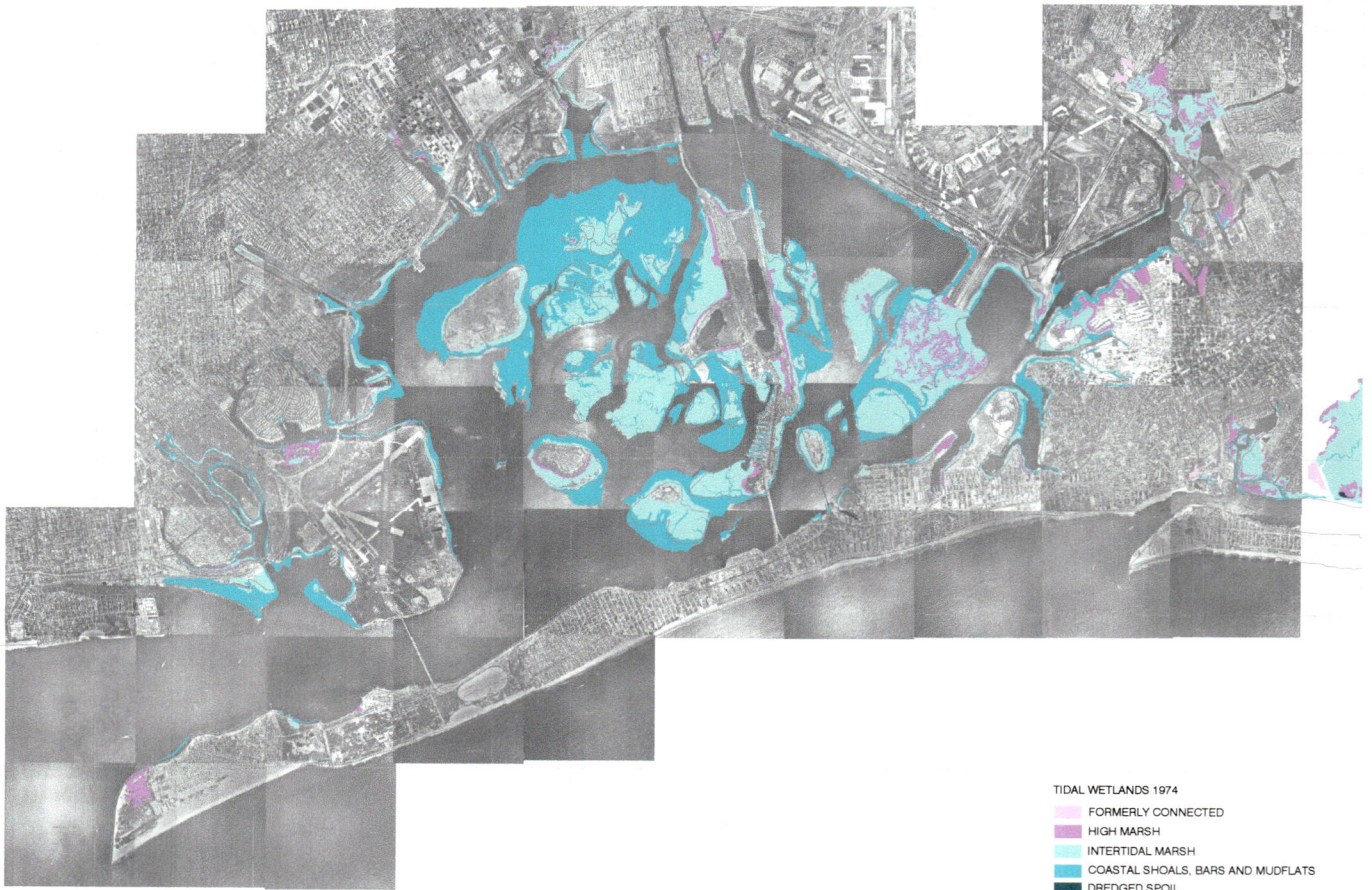

TIDAL WETLANDS 1974
- FORMERLY CONNECTED
- HIGH MARSH
- INTERTIDAL MARSH
- COASTAL SHOALS, BARS AND MUDFLATS
- DREDGED SPOIL

ENVIRONMENTAL VULNERABILITY TIDAL WETLANDS

data source: New York State Department of Environmental Conservation

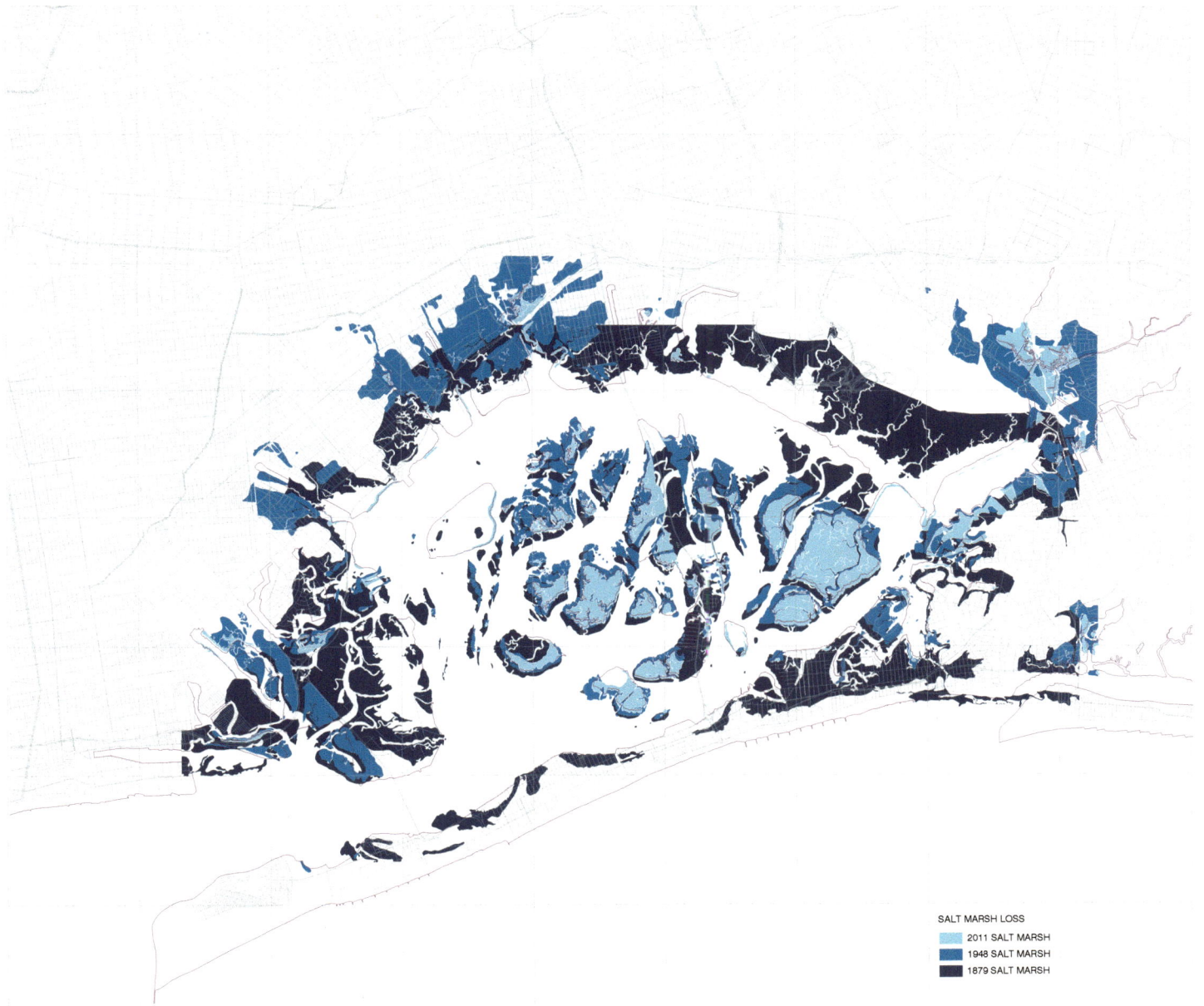

SALT MARSH LOSS 1879 - 2011

data source: National Oceanic and Atmospheric Administration

SALT MARSH LOSS

- 2011 SALT MARSH
- 1948 SALT MARSH
- 1879 SALT MARSH

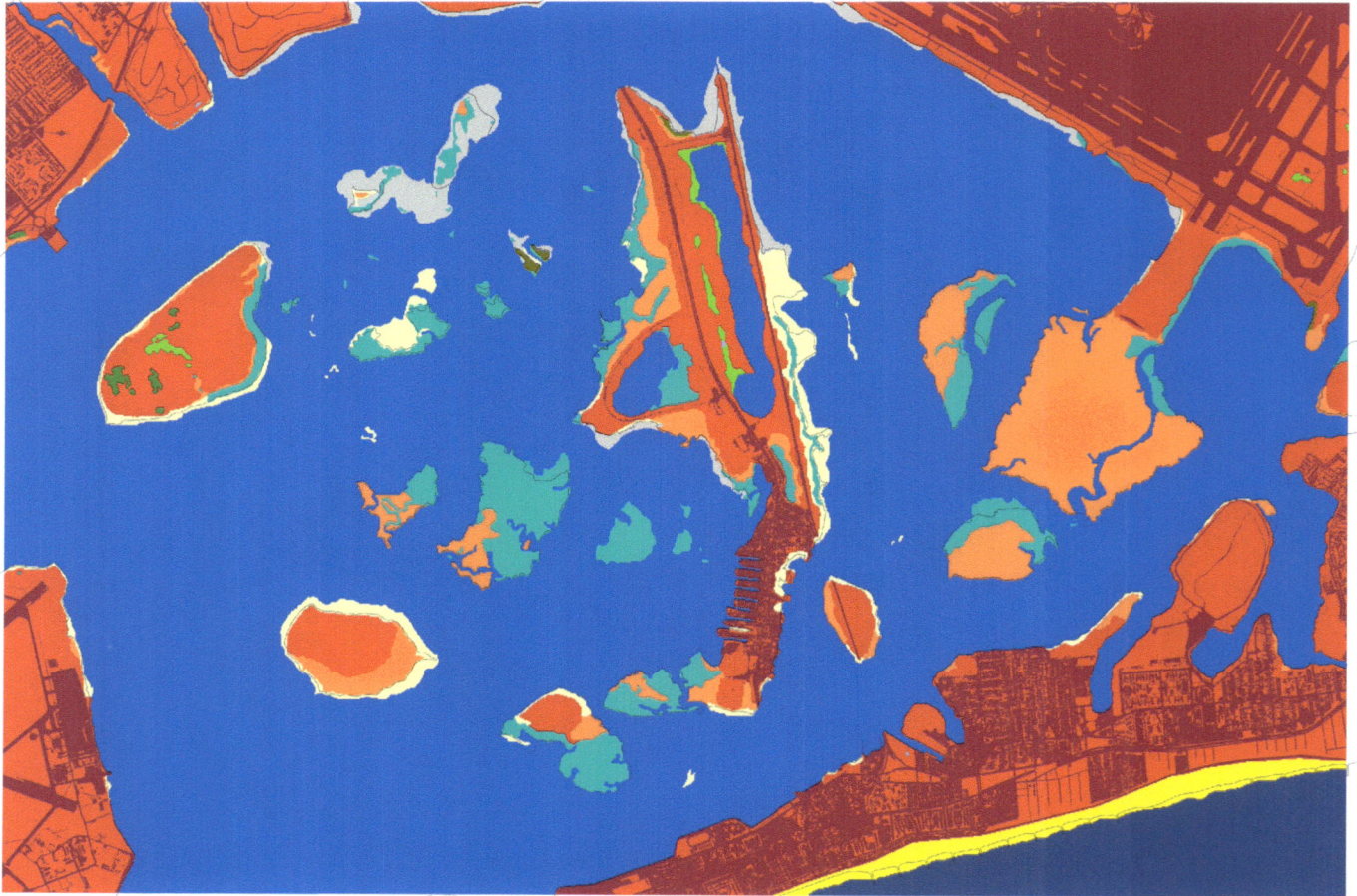

■ DEVELOPED DRY LAND	■ ESTUARINE BEACH
■ UNDEVELOPED DRY LAND	■ TIDAL FLAT
■ SWAMP	■ OCEAN BEACH
■ INLAND FRESH MARSH	■ INLAND OPEN WATER
■ TIDAL FRESH MARSH	■ TIDAL CREEK
■ TRANS. SALT MARSH	■ INLAND SHORE
■ REGULARLY FLOODED MARSH	■ TIDAL SWAMP

2014 (existing conditions)

ENVIRONMENTAL VULNERABILITY SEA LEVELS AFFECTING MARSH MIGRATION (SLAMM) MODEL

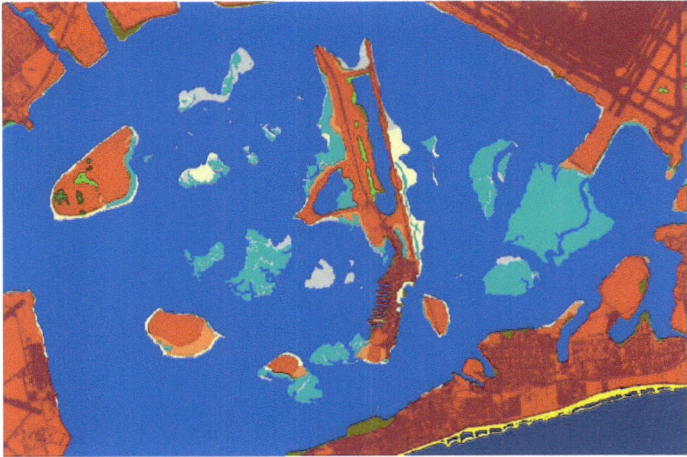

2025

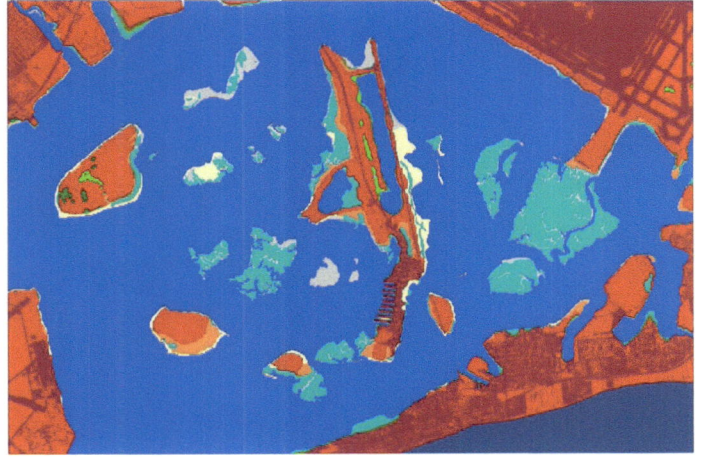

2050

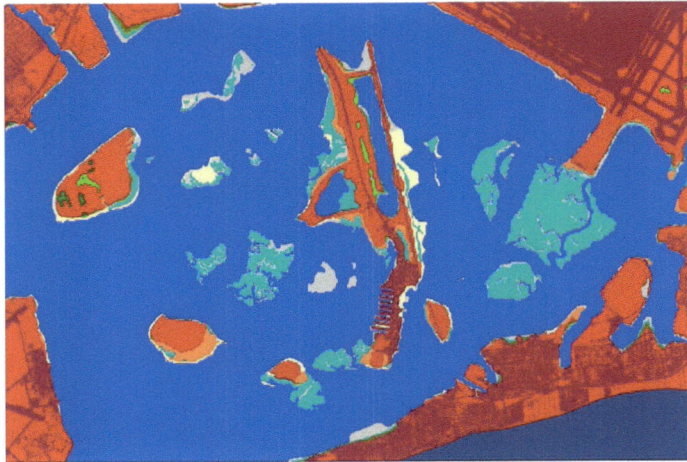

2075

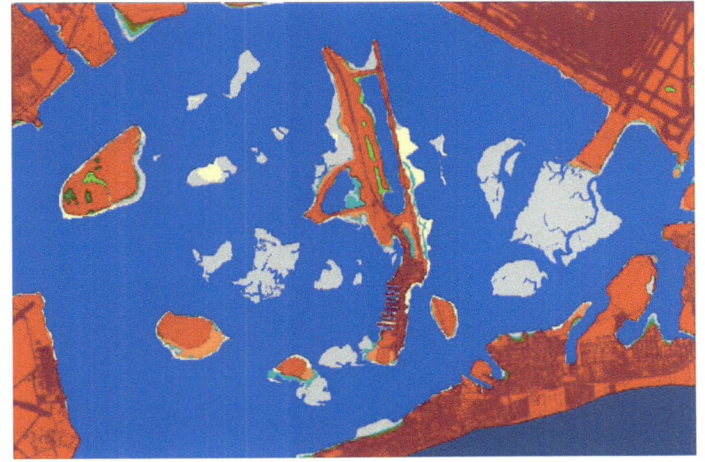

2100

data source: Warren Pinnacle Consulting, Inc.

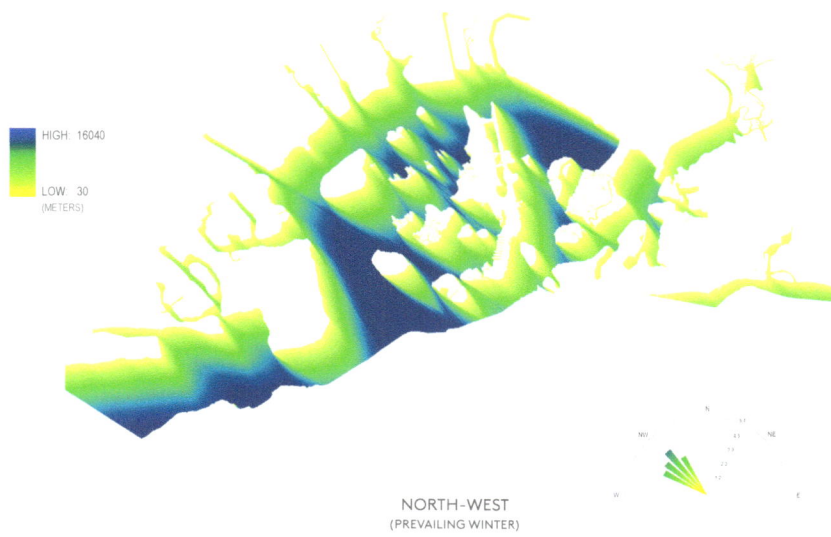

HIGH: 16040

LOW: 30
(METERS)

NORTH-WEST
(PREVAILING WINTER)

HIGH: 15680

LOW: 30
(METERS)

SOUTH
(PREVAILING SUMMER)

ENVIRONMENTAL VULNERABILITY WIND FETCH - WAVES2012

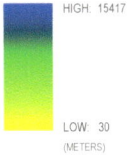

HIGH: 15417

LOW: 30
(METERS)

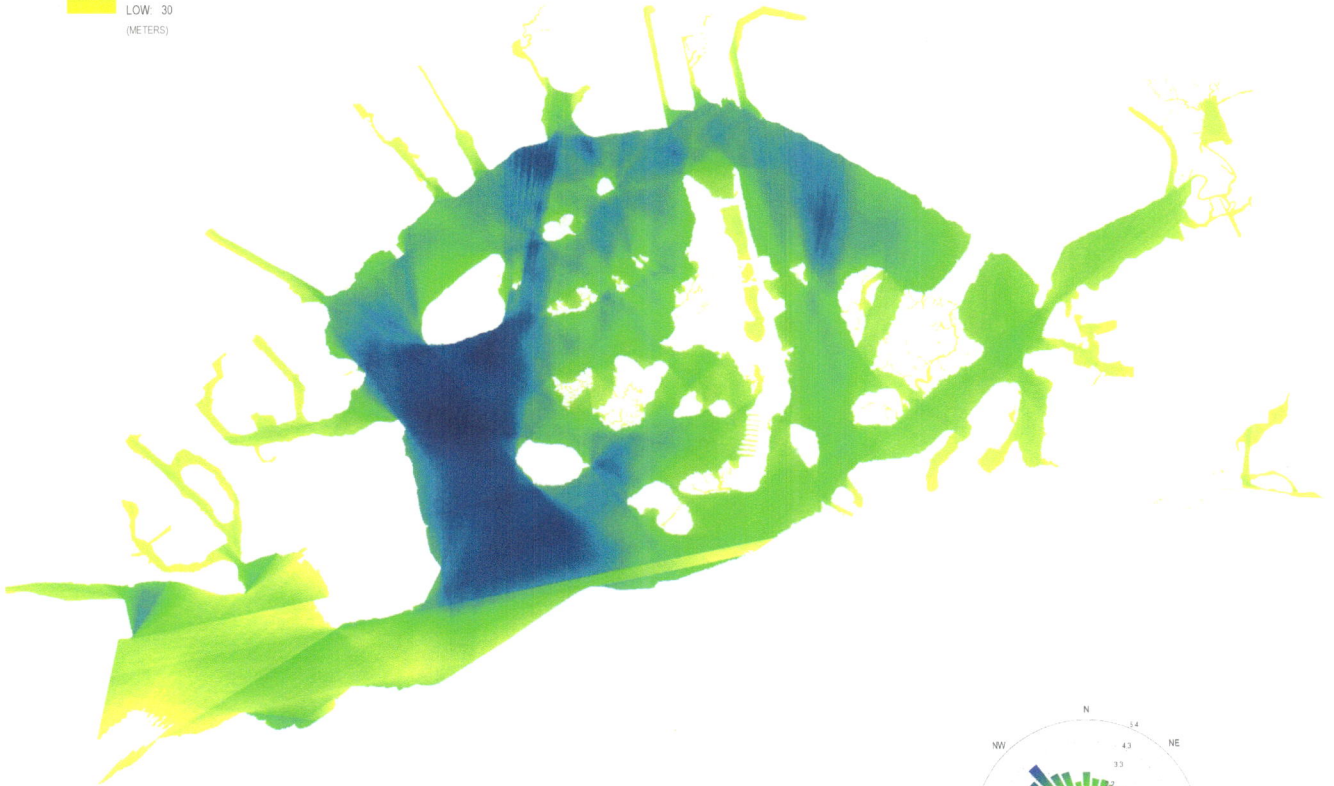

WEIGHTED SUM

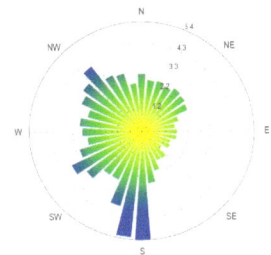

wind rose data source for JFK Airport: http://mesonet.agron.iastate.edu/sites/windrose.phtml?station=JFK&network=NY_ASOS

ENVIRONMENTAL VULNERABILITY NASA LANDSAT SATELLITE IMAGERY: VEGETATION CHANGE 1975-2010

VEGETATION CHANGE 2005-2010

data source: USGS and NASA

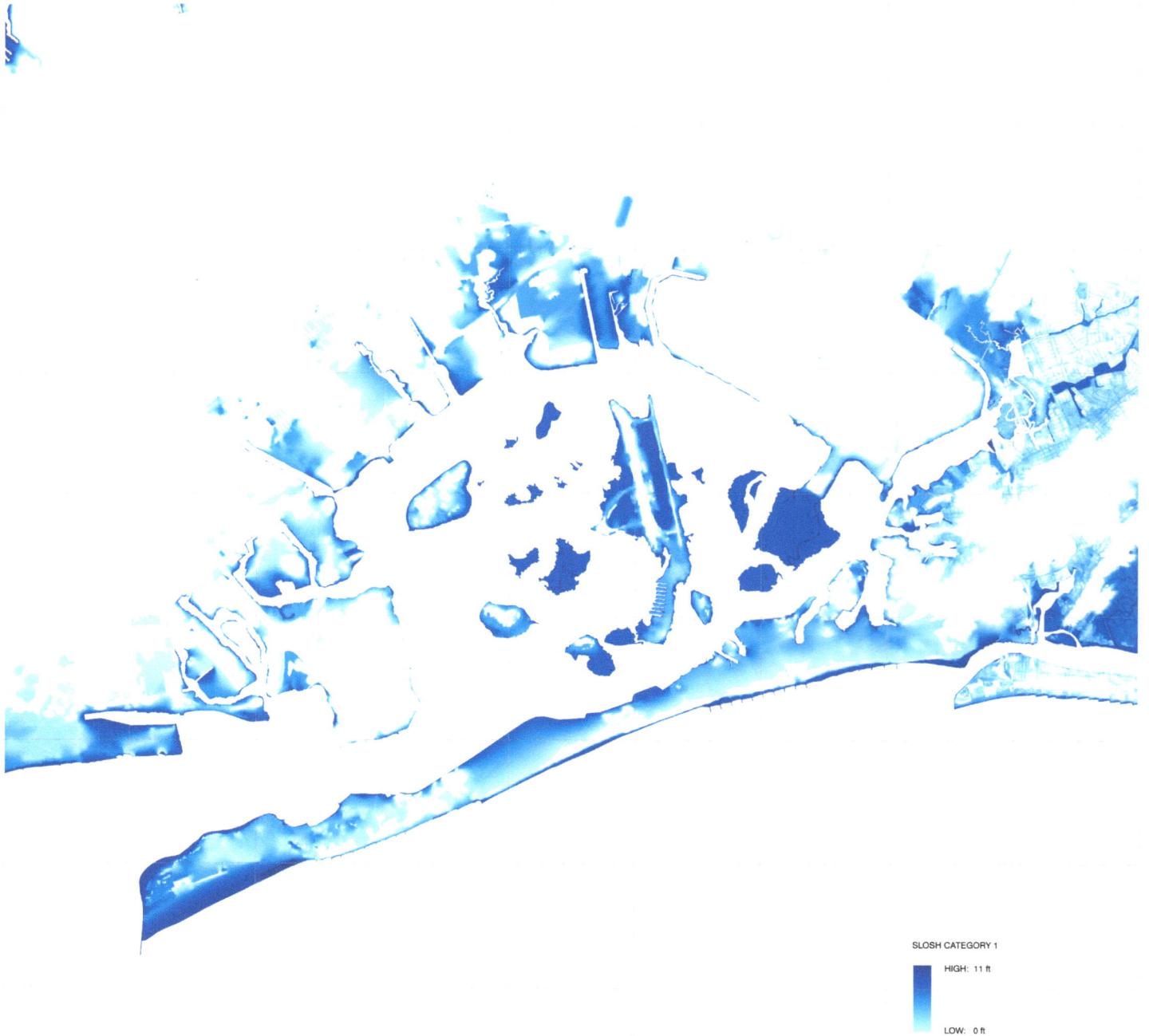

SLOSH CATEGORY 1

HIGH: 11 ft

LOW: 0 ft

ENVIRONMENTAL VULNERABILITY SEA, LAKE, AND OVERLAND SURGES FROM HURRICANES (SLOSH): Maximum Envelope of Water

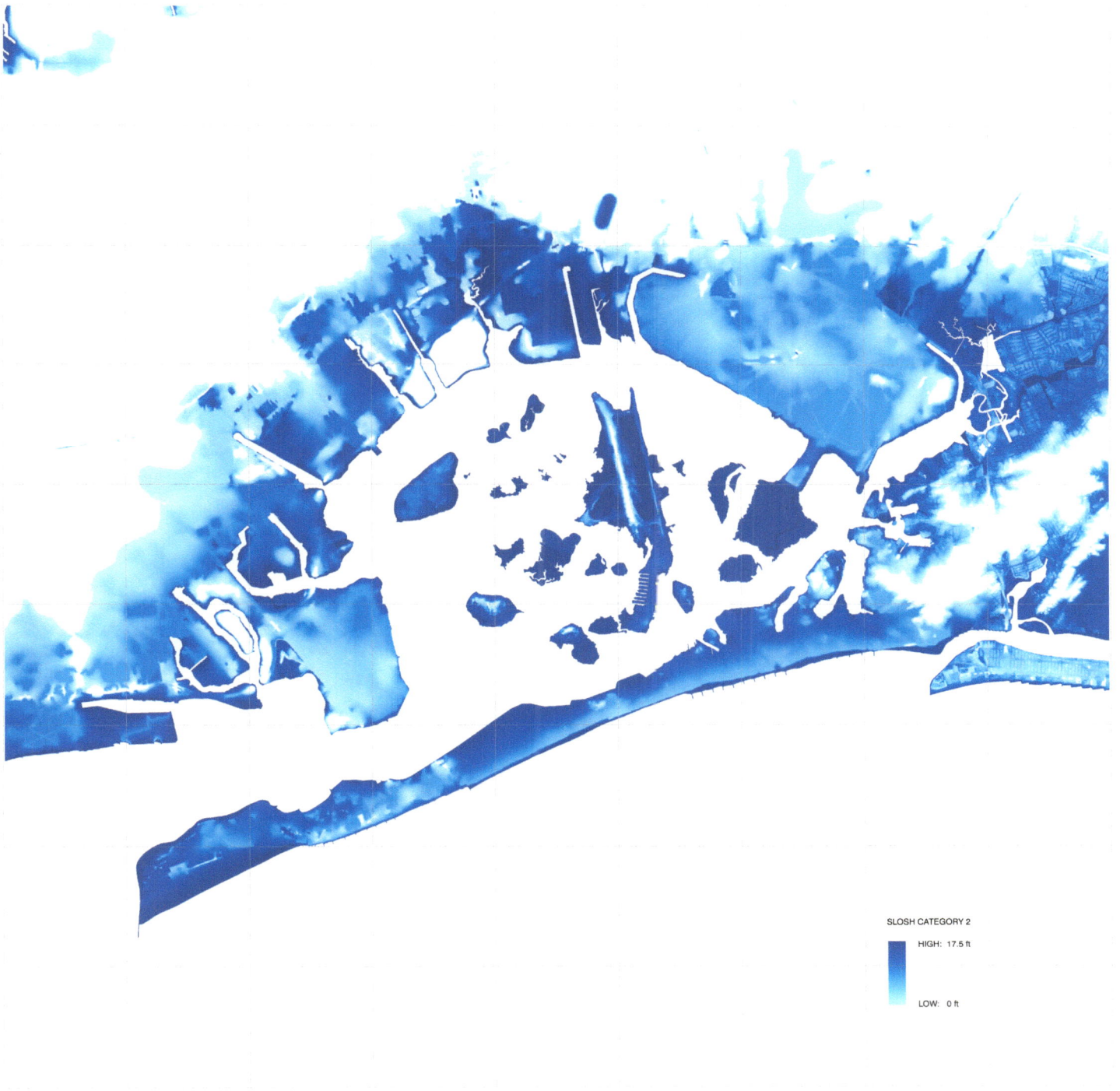

SLOSH CATEGORY 2

HIGH: 17.5 ft

LOW: 0 ft

data source: National Oceanic and Atmospheric Administration

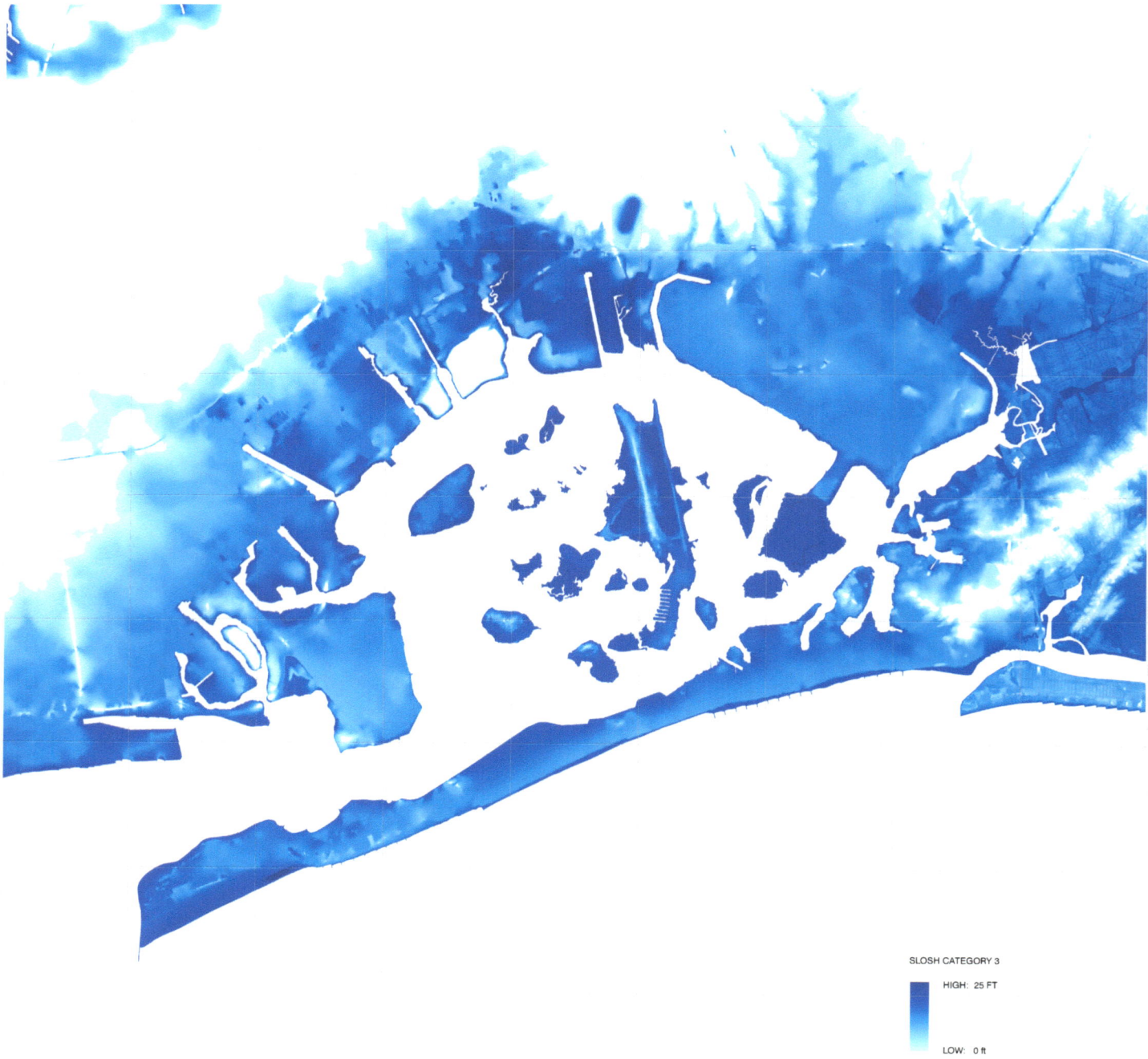

SLOSH CATEGORY 3

HIGH: 25 FT

LOW: 0 ft

ENVIRONMENTAL VULNERABILITY SEA, LAKE, AND OVERLAND SURGES FROM HURRICANES (SLOSH): Maximum Envelope of Water

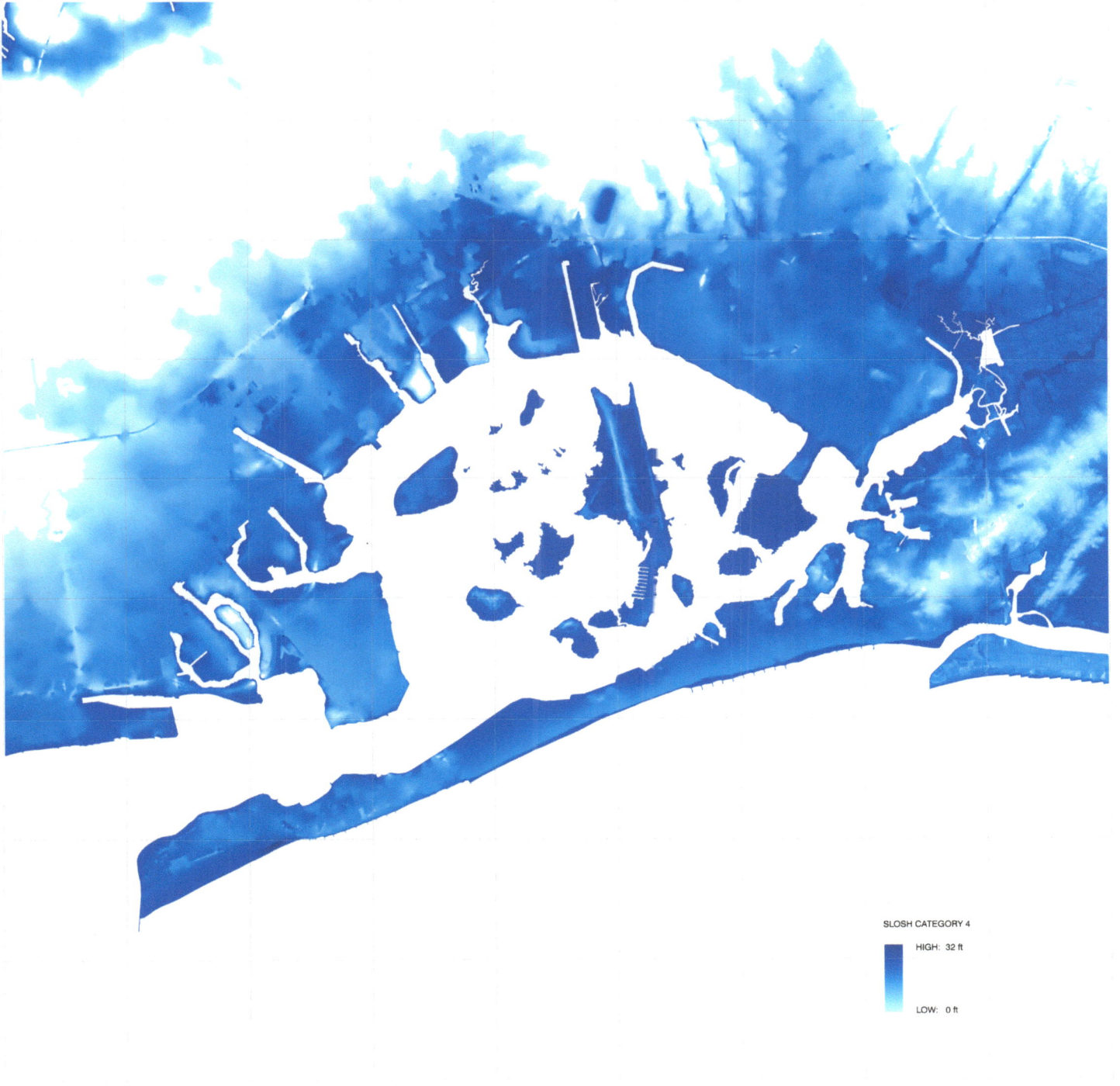

SLOSH CATEGORY 4

HIGH: 32 ft

LOW: 0 ft

data source: National Oceanic and Atmospheric Administration

INFRASTRUCTURAL VULNERABILITY AT JAMAICA BAY

The communities in and around Jamaica Bay host significant infrastructural assets. In addition to remnants from the region's history as an industrial processing and dumping zone, Jamaica Bay currently has four active wastewater treatment plants, three recently closed sanitary landfills, a power generation station, myriad fuel storage tanks, and one of the world's busiest airports, John F. Kennedy International Airport. Protection of transportation infrastructure is critical at Jamaica Bay, particularly given the region's dependence on these corridors as emergency evacuation routes. The Cross Bay Boulevard, the Marine Parkway-Gil Hodges Memorial Bridge, and the Nassau Expressway all lead out of the city's evacuation zones. Smaller-scale social infrastructure such as police stations, fire stations, medical centers, and schools become important nodes for gathering, communication, and resource distribution for those unable or unwilling to evacuate. Both the evacuation arteries and these smaller notes need protection in order to provide refuge, relief, and recovery support.

Rockaway Surf Club as a post-Sandy distribution center, November 2012
photo: Chris Tackett for Tree Hugger

INFRASTRUCTURE ASSETS AND VULNERABILITY

Legend:

- Power Supply
- P — Police
- H — Hospital
- h — Local Medical Center
- F — Fire Station
- School
- Evacuation Center - 1 and 2 Mile Radius

- Water Pollution Control Plant
- Water Pollution Control Plant Outfall
- Sewershed
- Potable Water Facility

- Natural Gas Pipeline
- Rail Line
- Major Road

Hurricane Evacuation Zones
- Zone 1
- Zone 2
- Zone 3
- Zone 4
- Zone 5
- Zone 6

Concrete sea wall protecting Neponsit, Rockaway Peninsula, 2013
photo: Danae Alessi

Rainbow dredging for Big Egg Marsh restoration, c. 2003
photo: Don Riepe

Rockaway Beach
photo: Don Riepe

Fish kill near the Jamaica Bay Wildlife Refuge, c. 1991
photo: Don Riepe

John F. Kennedy Airport runway, 2014
photo: Danae Alessi

E. F. Barrett Power Station, 2014
photo: Danæ Alessi

Cross Bay Veterans Memorial Bridge and A Subway train trestle, 2014
photo: Danae Alessi

Gil Hodges Memorial Marine Parkway Bridge, Rockaway Inlet, c. 1996
photo: Don Riepe

www.ingramcontent.com/pod-product-compliance
Lightning Source LLC
Chambersburg PA
CBHW060826270326
41931CB00002B/78